BORDER CROSSINGS

By Christopher Hampton

POETRY:
An Exile's Italy (Stuart Thonnesen, 1972)
A Cornered Freedom (Peterloo, 1980)
Against the Current (Katabasis, 1995)
Edited:
Poems for Shakespeare 1 (Globe Playhouse Trust, 1972)
Poems for Shakespeare 6 (Globe Playhouse Trust, 1978)

PROSE:
Island of the Southern Sun, novel for children (Chatto and Windus, 1962)
The Etruscans, art and culture (Gollancz, 1969)
Socialism in a Crippled World, politics and literature (Penguin, 1981)
The Ideology of the Text, politics and literature (Open University Press, 1990)

ANTHOLOGY:
A Radical Reader: The Struggle for Change in England 1381-1914, prose and poetry, as editor with historical commentary throughout (Penguin, 1984)

TRANSLATED:
The Fantastic Brother, by René Guillot (Methuen, 1961)

Border Crossings

Poems

Christopher Hampton

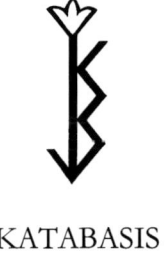

KATABASIS

First published in October 2005
by KATABASIS
10 St Martin's Close, London NW1 0HR (020 7485 3830)
katabasis@katabasis.co.uk
www.katabasis.co.uk
Copyright © Christopher Hampton 2005
Cover painting and design: Richard Downer
Printed by CLE Print, Media House, Burrel Road, St Ives,
Huntingdon PE27 3LE (01480 465233)
Typeset in-house mainly in 12 point Garamond.

ISBN 0 904872 41 6
Trade Distribution: Central Books
99 Wallis Road
London E9 5LN
(020 8986 4854)

British Library Cataloguing in Publication Data:
A catalogue record for this book is available
from the British Library.

Contents

I. Into the New Millennium

11 The Right Words
12 What it Means to Speak
13 The Unutterable
14 February 2001
15 Balked Flight
16 The Imperatives of Promise
17 On Days Like This
18 The Anonymous Makers
19 Bedfordshire Sunset
20 Socialism
21 Question and Answer
22 Justice
23 The Bottom Line
24 Prologue to War
25 Operation Infinite Justice
26 Beyond the Birds
27 On Lauren Slater's *Opening Skinner's Box*
29 *I* is an Other
30 April the First 2003
31 The Night Sky
32 Voices
33 What Remains Unsaid
35 Fast-Track Change

II. Speaking for the Future

39 Portrait of Sir Philip Sidney
40 Rosa Luxemburg at Wronke
41 Georg Lukács
42 Transformations

43 Death of a Poet
45 Resilience Beyond Defeat
46 Remembering Allende's Chile
47 Neruda: Fruits of the Sun
48 Heinrich Heine
50 Kazantzakis in Iraklion
52 The Witch of Vori
53 The Mesara Valley, Vori

III. Out of the Past

57 Illusions
58 Competitive Industry
60 A Former Citizen Speaks his Mind
62 Paschal to his Queen
64 Limbo Church
67 The Toll
69 Not of Siestas
70 A Letter at Dusk
71 The Aftermath
73 Affirmatives
74 Question of Truth's Absence
75 No-Man's Land
76 Islands of the Mind
78 Caliban
79 Witnesses
81 What Survives
82 Things Taking their Course
84 A Country Millimetres Deep
86 The Invitation

Acknowledgements

A poem from *Border Crossings* has been broadcast on BBC *Poetry Now*. Others have appeared in the journals *Acumen, Critical Quarterly, Literary Review, New York Times, Poetry Now, Poetry One, sof, Transatlantic Review, Tribune,* and *In the Company of Poets*, an anthology edited by John Rety (Hearing Eye, 2003).

I

Into the New Millennium

The Right Words

You're going to have to conjure the words
from the back of the mind, the dark of the throat,
as birds do by instinct, startling the dawn
with a music as effortless as the movement
of air or the coming of light. But how to manage that,
to pitch the notes the way such instinct works?
It isn't so easy. Making a music of words,
where ecstasy is speechless, means learning to speak
the comradeship of silence, where the music starts.
You cannot ever make words witnesses
until you've got to the heart of what gives birth
to speech. It's disciplined passion's the secret;
stress that speaks and strikes and takes the strain
of what's outside the frame and makes it sing;
till even the abstracts are part of the song.

What it Means to Speak

Make it an exclusive language then,
with words that have no echoes but our own,
revealing things that no-one else can say,
the inexpressible made sayable.

Ridiculous of course. This language
has no words that are not shared.
And what you make of it is others' too,
a coinage learnt from scratch to serve
a million causes, used and used,
the worn and echo-sounding syllables
that murmured at you in the womb –
a sonic whisper, a vibration
that you have to make speak sense,
even if to no-one but yourself.

And maybe we can only celebrate
what's ours by not forgetting
where it comes from, what it means
to speak an ancient ravaged tongue.

The Unutterable

The unutterable is unutterable!
Beauty means the way you feel,
is when delight and passion meet,
and breaking through reserves in sensate
quickening, lays its hold on you
to take possession. Speechlessly
you recognise, and let it speak,
at best by touch, when lip and tongue
are otherwise engaged.
That cliché exclamation at the sunset
may be just about the most
that we can do if not by painting it
or (better still) creating parallels
with music's liquid shimmering.

But now I'm groping not for sunsets
but for what it is
comes out of the unutterable
to make the poem speak
with something of the lucid magic
of a Titian nude,
a Mozart or a Mahler song.

February 2001

Take that twenty-year-old walnut tree
settled there beyond the kitchen window,
thrusting leafless branches to the sky.
It's a safer bet than poetry.
It lays no claims to permanence,
and like the face of the Tollund Man
knows nothing of the appeal it makes
to the future – time unravelling in slow
and leathered proof, where last year's fruit
dropped black stained casings in the grass,
and left no other trace but the nuts,
some two years old, still waiting to be cracked,
and like the Tollund Man intact –
though *he* sleeps on, brows knitted,
skin stained walnut-black by peat,
through centuries of troubled calm,
the dark of his undeciphered dream.

Balked Flight

I read slowly, taking the weight of the words,
breathing them through, sensing around me
the labour of growth and decay.
This music floats above the stripped Winter
where, displayed again beneath evaporating snow,
the ground's detritus and its hidden fruit
make embryonic gestures to the coming Spring.
I let my own words loose to take the stress
of all they move across the surface of –
ideas and feelings nurtured on distress
that check and turn like winter birds in flight.
But finding nothing – in the end reduced to mute
foreclosure – I myself am forced to turn back,
knowing, like an atheist in an empty church
caught listening for voices in a fruitless search
for answers, I can make no more of what I see,
the mind's quest balked by this complexity,
than what these tentative groping words betray.

The Imperatives of Promise

So take it up again. What waits in silence
through the tragedies of history, in the broken mists,
beyond the doorstep, out below the planets,
where the questions beckon, is the key: the word-game.
Play it cool, play deep, play hard, make patterns
count in the thrust of dispute and disjunction;
bring together what in a century of betrayals
pulls apart – these broken imperatives of promise
that have driven millions to crisis and despair.
It's not an option. There are words that cross the frontiers
of hope and failure, to challenge the violence
that isolates and make it possible to act
against the operators of the killer-systems
we have helped to put in place. And what they start from
is refusal, stubbornness of quest, insistence
on the fundamentals of distinction by which
fuses are lit that might begin to bring back light
to a darkened and damaged universe.

On Days Like This

On days like this you do not need
the voices of philosophers to help you
reconcile the ugliness, where the hate-seed
grows and it seems there's no way through
to the other side of the power-game.
On days like this it's sudden Spring
and everything's a new green no-name
shock to the senses, and there's no such thing
as privatisation or profit on health.
But who all the same's in any state
to ignore the doubts that come by stealth,
or the questions that by-pass those who wait?

The Anonymous Makers

Arrington, Cambridgeshire

Out of the nameless places of their birth,
under the tutelage of a classless sun,
these people have emerged in their millions.
Note them where they've left their mark,
where, everywhere at work, these hands
have coaxed the earth to fruitfulness.
The credit may have gone to others,
individuals abusing power
to build positions for themselves
and rise upon the backs of the anonymous.
But here you sense the presence in the fields
of what these nameless men and women did.
The air is vibrant with the record of it,
visible and interlinked, a wordless book
that leaves ambiguous proofs of the narrative –
an epic that reveals itself through every curve
and layer after layer of the yields of earth –
transformed, reformulated, sealed away.

Bedfordshire Sunset

I listen for it, for the signals
that flicker at me from a secret world,
sounds quivering with life,
where there beyond the garden wall
the red brush flares and the sky
burns into the linear silences
of Bedfordshire. What is it
comes from the heart of that fire,
that sense of animal heat
in the depths of the sharpening black,
like voices out of the stillness
and the bronze – a distant music,
hands that beat and slap
from somewhere far beyond this place
that speak the common struggle,
linking this Bedfordshire
sunset to the colours and sounds
of an anguished continent?
                              I hear it:

Hands that reach out cannot heal
nor words weighed out like bread
give hope to those who have no bread.

Socialism

In the Wake of New Labour

Why can't we speak of it now –
now that the summer's come,
bringing with it renewed adrenalin
as the flowers put their banners out?
Why does it have to be whispered about
as if it were some arcane joke?
The flowers don't apologise –
given light and air they celebrate.
But we have been seduced
by the market's plastic flowers;
have sold our voices out
that used to speak so unashamedly
of what so many fought so hard for.

Why can't we speak of it now
with the confidence of summer flowers?

Why do we have to apologise
to those who've swamped us into silence,
trampled all our banners down, made millions
out of what their brokers conjure from the air
in a drench of ground-polluting wealth?

Question and Answer

So what kind of voice do we have to have
to get the message through?
Just turn your back, just turn your back.

No, listen! What I'm saying is
we cannot let this go. Can you?
Just turn your back, just turn your back.

But that's no answer. Let it all go?
That's what they *want* us to do.
Just turn your back, just turn your back.

So you believe no answer's best –
to shrug one's shoulders and ignore it all?
Yes, turn your back, just turn your back.

But that would leave them in control.
Is that what you want? Is that what you want?

It makes no difference. Fight – you lose.
We have no power. It's they who choose,
control the ground, hold all the weapons.
Turn your back, just turn your back.

But doing that's against all sense,
all common ground, all shared experience.
We cannot let them get away with that.

But look at the facts, just look at the facts!
They've sewn it all up – technology's
global magic puts the market out of reach.
So turn your back, just turn your back.

Justice

You hear the word as a whispered plea,
a small explosion in the dark,
an asterisk stain on the black of space.

You cannot see the face.
There's no-one there to answer back.

The Bottom Line

How close can the poet get to the bottom line?
Manoeuvring, distancing, flinching away;
sitting perplexed by words in a New York dive;
getting too close to the bared self to say
too much about what others suffer at the unsafe
bottom line of poverty where money's life;
walking the tightrope of the Ireland war;
watching it break in Rwanda and Bosnia;
probing the silence for a voice that will drive
through doubt to break the deadlocked, raw
conditioning that undermines all will to speak?

Prologue to War

'The kaleidoscope has been shaken. The pieces are in flux. Soon they will settle again. Before they do, let us re-order this world around us.' –
TONY BLAIR, Labour Party Conference Speech, 2nd October 2001

This is what transcendence does to us.
It brings about the triumph of the cloaked,
the invisible, the unaccountable,
over that which can be brought to book.
Things driven by the god-obsessed
and their so-called godless enemies
sweep aside the human context
even as the hidden hand of profit does.
Now, with the moral order of the West
assuming beneficent control of the just
against the absolutes of Islam,
the politics of transcendence float above
the brutal politics of hatred and death.
And how are we to treat this high-altitude
language of the liberal conscience pitting
compassion against force, and telling us,
even as the bombers move in on Kabul,
'the values we believe in should shine through
whatever we do in Afghanistan.'

Operation Infinite Justice

Later renamed 'Enduring Freedom' –
War Force: 2001

Justice as infinite as this
comes crude as the rhetoric
that echoes the Islamic
absolutes it sets itself against.
What hope can any of us have,
working for an unfenced
world, by pilfering words from above
to answer finite crime with justice?
We've no right to the Infinite. This,
if it's God's law, isn't for us.
We inhabit a muddier ground,
unfit for any God-like unbound
all-seeing presence in the sky.
Ensnared by terrorist certainty,
which murders in the name of God,
we have to ask who set the trap
that unleashed terror if not those
who for decades had milked the poor
to the very limits of despair.
The absolutes of Islam and the West,
equating the Higher Truths they claim
with Justice, are equally to blame.
Where ideologies meet head on,
it's people are the losers, trapped between:
New York, Washington, Afghanistan.

Beyond the Birds

*During Sharon's assault on the refugee cities of the West Bank –
1st May 2002*

I sit listening in comfort to the birds
in a garden orchestrated by the backdrop
of the May sun's flowers and trees.
There is an ominous counterpoint to this though,
out of sight two thousand miles away,
where other birds might still be singing,
somewhere in the hanging gardens of the Jenin camp –
where, trapped beneath the rubble of their houses,
there are children who might never sing again.
I hear them, this catastrophe beyond the birds,
these broken voices choked by the gun-smoke
of the helicopter gun-ships overhead,
that put an end to hope for those who can't fight back.
And who is listening? And who that listens
has the power or the will to act against the silencers?

On Lauren Slater's *Opening Skinner's Box*

St. Leomer, Vienne, France

I read of a child crying at night;
of a dog howling 'soap-white in the moonlight';
of 'the sky outside... generously salted with stars'.
The images are Lauren Slater's; and I take them on
to make of them the luminous immediacy
she'd lighted up an unknown night with.
Nor do I rob her of the words she's coined.
They're hers still, even as I seek to make them mine,
against the red of the prunus I look out on
backed by the yellow in the green of the oaks
and the hidden song-struck nightingales.
Beyond me, in time, is the moonlit night
I glance at, getting up at four
to answer a behavioural necessity;
before which was the dinner-table talk,
of wine and food and children – journeys
down through France made fifty years ago,
which brought up Wordsworth's walking tour
through revolutionary France in 1790.
Not the politics – all that remained unspoken,
the exhilarate salt of struggle, there in almost every word
in a world that's moved inexorably on
from what one might have hoped would give us
'human nature seeming born again' –
the illusion that it could: make 'social life,
through knowledge spreading and imperishable,
as just in regulation, and as pure,
as individual in the wise and good'.
How could it? Murder, civil strife, the Terror –
now as then – what Wordsworth's disillusionment,
salt rubbed into the wounds of conscience,

was succeeded by. Like him 'we have to cry it out'
in order in the classic Skinner sense
to rid ourselves of such behaviour, if we can.
What our age is suffering from, he tells us,
'isn't our anxiety, but... wars, crimes, terror'
fuelled by men who want us acquiescent to their ends,
generating fear to stop us ever thinking
we can beat the killers and make human sense
of what we are. For they want servitude,
which soap-white *serves* their ends. They *don't* want
dignity and freedom, love, autonomy,
though this is what they *say* they do. The truth
might open up too many Skinner boxes,
put these people out of joint, and break the stranglehold
by which they keep us quiet, bought and sold.

B.F.Skinner (1903-1990), US psychologist, invented the 'Skinner Box', an enclosed environment for the observation of behavioural conditioning.

I is an Other

'Je est un autre' — RIMBAUD

There are ways of trying,
though the *I* a friend had argued for
in casual debate is not enough.
'Be careful,' I'd said.
'You have to match the singular
to all that lies outside it,
gives it meaning, makes it work.
There are conditions that determine
what this *I* can say or do.
Poetry, it's true, begins from the self,
but can't assume that what it speaks for
comes from nothing else. Beyond it
lie the voices it subsumes,
the history it's rooted in.

Take Mandelstam,
speaking for the dispossessed.
He as you and we and us,
the *I* that isn't them, makes moves
against the enemy within.
You see how vulnerable
this floating *I* can be,
attempting its autonomy as if
it had the power to stand alone
against the forces of the universe.'

April the First 2003

On April Fools' Day, after thirteen days of war,
one has to ask how many of us have been taken in.
Is this reality, this nightmare we're confronted with,
some shadowy bitter joke being played out
daily on our TV screens? You see the bombing
of the cities, and the tanks, the guns, the twisted bodies.
Is it foolish to be thinking murder's been let loose?
Our trusted representatives are talking 'liberation tactics'.
We are in Iraq, it seems, to free the people
from a hateful tyrant. This at least's the weasel version
that is trotted out to reassure the doubters,
even as they drop their fools'-day booby-traps,
their cluster bombs and Cruises into the laps
of those too innocent to understand.
And if the scattered cluster bomblets blind,
that is done in all good faith – missiles, bombs and mines
are seedlings for democracy. They open up the lines
of contact, Middle East from Middle West –
Spring's message: the US/UK Bush-Blair test.
'We've hearts and minds to win and markets to invest,
and liberty to offer at its cruellest best.'
So now this April Fools' Day's had its way,
perhaps (they'll say) it's time to put the dead to rest
and turn to welcome the unwelcome US guest.

The Night Sky

You'll make no new discoveries tonight.
The moon's an absence: gone to China.
Look outside – there's nothing there to inspire
but black silence and the stabbing lights
of a passing car that turn the walnut tree
to shuttered negative under the Great Bear,
now tilted up to advertise the Pegasus Square,
with Cygnus raised like a crucifix
above the southern shadow of an unseen pear.
These are nothing new. The night-sky's clichés
make no talking-points: you recognise
in this confusion only its familiar pattern,
punctuating silence with unanswering light,
which comes to haunt a thousand years too late,
and leaves us doubting whose this future is
we sense there sinking down beyond the hills
as stillness blackens and the sky takes charge.

Voices

St. Leomer, Vienne, France –
April 2005

Speak the voices of the garden quiet
against post-modernist clamour.
Look for equivalents linked
from the swiftness of a Mozart ending
to the nightingale's night-notes
pitched against the darkness of C minor
in a long vibrating D that breaks
the rain's monotony. You hear it?
Listen! What it speaks of, riding
the choral ground-bass of the frogs,
we have no words for, there in the depths
of the garden oaks above the water,
singing hidden in the dark –
a Philomel unreconciled to crime:
the violated body, the revenge,
the punishment; of all of which
throughout the Spring – day/night – she sings.

What Remains Unsaid

For my mother

1

No answers can ever suffice.
If they break the spell of the ice
of silence that cuts her off from us,
they touch the freezing waters of the sea
of death beneath as she turns her head
to look at me.
          There's nothing to be said.
Her hands, her wilted body, tilted, bent,
are proof enough, the eyes intent.
She speaks through silence, and her mute
appeal from the dying self – this absolute
that hovers close – comes distant, puzzled
out of a daze of love, a muzzled
longing. 'Tell me, tell me.'
                    But we know
I cannot. And I have to let it go.

2

Remembering, thinking backward,
discovering the congealed
failed moment, the unhealed
wound in the lie, is tarnish
of death to the senses –
hurt of what remains unsaid,
ache of the lost and dead.

I look for the deeper voice
that cuts across the temporal

and comes from the roots like grass,
perennially fresh; and listen,
there beside my mother,
watching like an alien other
as her life turns inward,
hunched upon itself, an end
I cannot speak for or defend;

but sense, beyond this failure,
what remains from a lifetime
undefeated, things that last –
integrity and courage, trust
of womanhood, unjudging love:
it's these, the unsayable, survive.

Fast-Track Change

St. Leomer, Vienne, France – 29th March 2004

Make what you can of it then with words,
to match the colours of the Spring.
Here, while it's here, while they last,
with so much gone already – winter's rains,
the cold, the loss of leaves, the frost.
Gone at the turn of the head,
as if days were hours, the months days;
like water in the wake of the storms
that, racing through, have also gone –
breaking the banks of the Salleron,
flooding the fields and the pool
at the end of the garden, as in dream.
Except that these storms
have left their mark on the land,
left sandbanks exposed,
and there at the curve of the river,
a great split oak brought crashing down.

So make what you can of it now;
and as the dark takes over,
blackening the oaks and the celandine
yellows massed below,
speak for the clarity of the stars
at their galactic distance
above the slope of the garden
where they have so long stabbed
skies beyond the reach of thought.

And when the light returns,
to bring the colour back to Spring,
make what you can of it then, if you can.

II

Speaking for the Future

Portrait of Sir Philip Sidney

From a black and white postcard

You get nothing from this portrait, almost –
gaze of small eyes quick perhaps to see,
a mouth effeminately pursed, the ghost
of an intelligence. Not enough to set him free.

It leaves us with too many questions. He –
so rich with gifts, the witty stellar maker,
struck down, gone to earth – can here be
present for us only as a pale-faced joker,

teasing, teasing. But through words the seeker
stirs; from loving letters comes the friend,
the poet-patron of a great decade, and speaker
for renaissance, feted even to his Arnhem end.

Rosa Luxemburg at Wronke

October 1916 until July 1917

To be free to think and dream
as she walks the rain
in Madam Kautsky's cloak.
To feel as much at home
with the green of her plants
as ever she'd been on the battlefield
of European politics.
The world was there with her of course –
that murderous world
she'd walked the tightrope of
through all the jugglings of expediency,
up to the edge with the SPD
and its war-credit sell-out.

Listen! When I get back
there'll be no more meetings,
clandestine or otherwise!
I'll take my stand
in the thick of the action
where the wind roars in the ears.
I've had enough of talking.
What we need's commitment,
getting at the roots, making things new!

Now though it's back to my plants!

Georg Lukács

What Lukács struggled to articulate
in the flux and thrust of history,
dragging him out of contemplative
disquisition on the ethical arcane
into the cauldron heat of politics,
we have as our inheritance –
so many dead, the ravaged witnesses
to eight intolerable decades;
commitment broken into by the dogmas
of irrationalists, the plausible schemes
of blinded will that plunged a crippled Europe
into murder in the aftermath of war.

All that and worse the nineteen-thirties
turned to nightmare – what for Lukács
(caught between two terrorist extremes)
demanded a control of concept and of fact
impossible to reconcile except by subterfuge
in face of Stalinist terror and its deadly jargon.
Walking tightropes he survived it all,
though many failed to, spinning in the dark off-track,
retreating, turning back, as madness
and its war-machine swept millions everywhere
into the irrationalist-killers' traps.

Today, beyond the wreckage of collapse,
utopias that now lie broken-backed,
sold out to money's globalised controls,
it's just as difficult to break the mould –
what Lukács argued for against this killer-
stranglehold by which the circus-masters
maintain power to keep us dispossessed.

Transformations

Leningrad – Eighty years on

Here we are in the aftermath.
It feels a little like
some sort of death.
Except that this
is too uncomfortable for death.
Listen – there are voices
shouting in the dark!
But no-one hears them
here within the flat horizons
of this Cambridgeshire November.
And there in that city
of the reassumed name
where the Aurora still lies anchored,
Lenin gestures into silence
from the forecourt of the Finland Station,
trapped in a rhetoric of stone
to a superseded cause.

Now Petrograd's bronze horseman
takes the centre-stage again –
there on the banks of the Neva,
with its twenty-five canals,
makes broken reflections
of the city's autocratic origins,
surviving the toppled effigies
of its Leningrad dead
as if they'd never existed.
There the Northern sun
picks out those golden pinnacles,
while here it sinks
in melancholy gesture
to a world's frustrated dreams.

Death of a Poet

In memory of Amelia Rosselli,
'caduta sulla linea di battaglia'

Suddenly it matters.
In the tragic incidence of death,
a body falling from a fifth-floor window
breaks the distances between us.
Now I recognise the voice;
but only now, too late,
I note the common ground we covered –
Rome and England, music, Italy,
the English language,
traced against the silences
that kept us all our lives
pursuing separate paths.
And in the counterpoint of struggle
is the sense of it, the calling,
the defiance of unreason –
always vulnerable, it seems,
to the torment and the trauma
of the seven-year-old who lost
her father, murdered by fascists.
This is what no words can answer,
what she plunged to death to silence,
violence against violence.
Not that I can speak for her in this –
her life's not mine, her death's
an act I can't make sense of.
And yet from the obituary
comes a phoenix voice
pitched bitterly against
the sordid histories
of post-war compromise

she'd had to live through,
haunted by her father's death,
defeat upon defeat.
It echoes back at us
the itineraries of hope
that she and others spoke for.
It's as if that voice had said:

We carry within us the dead,
defiant in their silences —
all who've had to witness
in a climate of betrayal
the inequities and thefts of capital.

Resilience Beyond Defeat

For Martin Bell, poet, died 1978

Listen: what survives of him from four decades!

It's good to know how much there is: the playfulness,
the gaiety, the sense of timing that makes language
speak the comic probity and hurt of the clown.
It compensates for all the chances that were missed
of recognition and of fame. In this bare room
the courage of a generation echoes at us
from the underlying melancholy of the verse –
a world betrayed, a future messed about with,
which 'the old gang' did its best to smash through war,
and then, when that was over, organised again –
'More utter,' as he said, 'but deadlier, deadlier still.'

So is it now too late to take the cudgels up
and fight the sods who held such courage back?

'For Christ's sake no,' he'd say; 'they didn't get me.'

That's about the measure of it. 'Listen, carry on!' –
Resilience beyond defeat.
                        And that's the way it has to be.

Remembering Allende's Chile

*After the 25th anniversary of the murder of Allende –
11th September 1973*

'On our side, on the side of the Chilean revolution, were the constitution and the law, democracy and hope.' – PABLO NERUDA: Memoirs

'Once again they want to stain my land with workers' blood, those who talk of liberty but whose hands are marked with guilt.'
         – VICTOR JARA: Vientos del Pueblo, summer 1973

Chile's forests, the long spined snowline of the Andes;
nitrate-deserts of the North; the glittering seas –
remote from Europe, it would seem. But something more
than just another client-state, chaotic, poor,
controlled by US power. Standing up in socialist
and open challenge to the profiteers and fascist
rulers planted in their midst – who, scurrying off
to safeguard banknotes, jewels, coins, could only scoff
at what had brought back justice, all they'd crossed.

Of course it couldn't last. Allende's Chile was no contest
for such enemies. The army and the CIA,
the jugglers of New York, a middle class in disarray,
soon struck with tanks and bombers to obliterate
this workers' President, this hated workers' state.

In other words, what puts respect for people's needs
above the killer instincts competition breeds
is not so easily achieved, where Pinochet,
his concentration camps, the ITT, the USA,
stand straddled on the body of Neruda's Chile.

Neruda: Fruits of the Sun

'Frutas de sol a todos los oscuros!'
— PABLO NERUDA: El Pueblo

Neruda's explosive gaiety and latin flair
are not for the pragmatism of this London air.
Such poets make their gestures to a world
that quickens with the promise of the unspoiled
silences of woods and seas. Beyond that Chilean
beginning in the southern rain, a million
possibilities declared themselves – Parral-born,
exploring rock and foliage for insects, drawn
to the river and the thunder of the ocean's call.

Sensations multiply through the rise and fall
of this exotic Spanish – continents of common
speech unite us in pursuit of warmth to summon
all that brings disparate worlds together,
celebrating what we share against the weather
of divisive laws that break us, keep us dulled.

It's not so easy here though, with the people lulled.
In a climate of opinion nourished on the logic
of the market-place, Neruda's suspect, and lethargic
Britain plods through all its beauty unimpressed
by songs like his – indifferent to the harsher needs
he speaks for, rooted close to what the future breeds.

Heinrich Heine

'I myself am of the people. I am not one of the seven hundred wise men of Germany. I stand with the great masses at the portals of their wisdom.'
— HEINE: Religion and Philosophy

Born Jewish with an English fighter's name —
All men, he said, *are either Jews or Greeks* —
his Hebrew conscientiousness
was early tempered to a sane
Hellenic vision of the real
embodied in the Goethean ideal.

But not to worship — more like Hermes:
quick, impatient, driven to appeal,
coming with his messages of outrage
to an aged and indifferent Zeus,
and turning back to take his stand
against the ancient prisons of the mind,
those institutions of the *status quo*
that kept men shackled and in thrall.

The world he saw as one vast hospital
created by the state's great umpires
and the Church's creeds, its holy vampires,
parasitic to the spirit's needs.

So he, defining his community,
proclaimed himself a fighter
in the freedom war for health,
and aimed his salvoes of barbed wit
against old evils chanted in the blood,
the rhetoric of fear and servitude.

This wasn't a war that he could win.
But Heine knew no new Jerusalem
could ever be much more than dream
unless we believed it could be won.

And in the end, with irony and laughter,
from his mattress grave
he turned that lightning wit of his
upon the so-called radicals
who, with their earnest watchwords
and their vision of a joyless future,
threatened to reduce
to their mechanic scope
the spirit's liberating city.

This was not what *he* had fought for –
his democracy demanded more, much more.
These petty bureaucrats could only ape
the arbiters of true community,
mocking the gods in caricature.

Kazantzakis in Iraklion

Refused his place below
among the lozenges and rectangles
of modern Iraklion,
he lies above the city –
the agnostic Cretan,
forging words for the harsh
unyielding struggles of a people
out of the stony soil
of mountain villages.

The white stone spells it out:
I've neither hope nor fear: I'm free.
For what these words define,
defiant to the death,
is what they leave behind –
the record of the books,
where words are like struck stones
enacting the explosive
energy of resistance
and of hope that pits itself
against the leaden weight
of superstition and despair.

As for the bare wood cross,
planted there under the free sky
beside the white stone plaque,
what can that be made to signify?

It speaks a bitter wisdom,
turning all we fight for here
to little more than shadow-play,
defeating even possibility.

Against it what the poet knows
is what his work survives –
a body undiminished,
taking on another kind of life
to challenge all that's settled,
speaking for the future
from the weathered silences of Crete.

The Witch of Vori

Vori: a village five miles from Phaistos, Crete

The witch on the roof-terrace
turns on her broomstick.
Spinning round beneath the sky,
she grips the handle of the stick
as if in search of her magnetic North,
but can't stop long enough to cast her spell –
it's Easter, and the bells disturb her.
Down from Psiloritis comes the word,
a whispered zephyr that sets up a drift
of sound – bells that answer bells,
the bleat of sheep, the cock-crow,
birds, and children's voices punctuated
by the firecrackers' intermittent dry
staccato: *Christos anesti! Christos anesti!*
This she cannot fathom, gets confused by,
spins and wavers, stops and spins,
points north, turns south, swings east,
seems desperate now for information.
No-one listens though. Suspended in mid-air,
left dangling on her string, she stares
bewildered over the rooftops,
cheeks puffed out in a grimace of dismay.

The Mesara Valley, Vori

Near Phaistos, Crete

Out beyond the white-walled village
it is not the sky that moves.
The mountains, closed across with cloud,
define the evening's Easter green,
this Cretan light that floods
the red-earth tracks with instant yellow
through the silvered smoke of olives.
Today is a movable feast,
its silences breathe in a drift of air
no words can match. The way it speaks,
as the mountain snowline breaks through cloud
to ride the air, creates a syntax
out of space, a measure for the eye
to chart the groundwork of the earth by.
All this happens within sight of the village,
where stone refracts the glaze of the sky,
and ancient signals place the valley,
make undecipherable sense of its white
silences under an all-inclusive blue.

III

Out of the Past

Illusions

Azay-le-Rideau

A poem that could stand like Azay's château,
poised in symmetry above the lake,
a form to make stone float: it seems too much to ask.
Even as the poem echoes back its content,
an illusion built upon illusion, a façade
reflecting a façade, the château
casts its spell upon us, rising splendid
from the water in a glittering display
of surfaces.
          But touch the stones and look.
If architects make marks on paper, calculate
the mathematics – stress and mass and weight,
blueprints costed to a client's means –
it's still the hands of workmen build,
manoeuvring numbered blocks of stone,
their bodies glistening with sweat;
what vision cannot do without – though Azay,
there among its trees in elegant retreat,
can shrug them off, assume autonomy,
and seem a presence conjured from the atmosphere
that stands detached from all except itself.

Competitive Industry

Lumb Bank, above Hebden Bridge, Yorkshire

On the ash-black slopes of the hill,
across from the grit-stone house
and the fields of paled grass
that tilt to the cleft and the tangled
ruins of the mill below,
winter holds its own still,
keeps March leafless,
checks the break of green.

Down by the bridge
a waterfall defines the spot
where handloom weavers worked
and wheels turned for cotton;
till the competition came
that broke this industry
and brought these mills to ruin.

There I walk the skirl of wind
and sheen of sun
between two mill-stacks;
and as light explodes
to lightning counterpoint
among the net of trees,
I tread what history's left
to the earth's slow thrust and shift –
now churned to black of mould
and loosened stone, where water
sweats the quarried overhang

beneath the hill and, brown
to the drama of its kick and curl,
the moor-stream races down
through the bedrock of the gulley
to a blackened Yorkshire town.

A Former Citizen Speaks his Mind

From the Etruscan city of Caere,
subjected to Rome in the 3rd century BC

They smile, talk down at us and make their plans.
They walk like owners through our streets,
and nod at those among us
whom they condescend to notice.

Now, almost the first to bend,
intoxicated by the sights of Rome,
defiled by cynic luxuries,
bribed into the slack, our leaders walk –
you see them? – with patrician swagger
down the streets, in togas, white and fat
from drinking Latin. And the dead we honoured,
what of them? Betrayed and shamed, left
locked in the damp. These people talk of reason,
leech us to their parasitic codes.
As they destroyed our confidence,
so we have acquiesced
in willing degradation of the rest.

Be living with them? Grovel
in the shadow of white togas, die
to Latin epitaphs? It is our shame –
to be forgotten, to forget, to let
ourselves be travestied by Roman laws
and Roman lies till there is nothing left –
except the dead, who watch us (drained of will)
become the coward lackeys of the Roman state.
And they must know that we'll have soon
forgotten even them.

O yes, I cling to vestiges –
alone, a battery of echoes, a castrated
echo in a eunuch world. But though I
still remember, can still speak and sing,
it is to no-one but myself. Watching
as this town parades its puppets,
I see no Etruscans who have faces
they can call their own. With them –
blank, white-fleshed and brainwashed –
walks their nothingness.

And I, unsexed, can only spit and sneer.
In Latin, citizen. In my bastard Latin.

Paschal to his Queen

On the orders of Pope Paschal I, Santa Maria in Domnica, Rome, was rebuilt in the 9th century during the iconoclastic disputes.

She stares from her deep sky,
my enthroned blue queen.
I am the dwarf
kneeling at her feet.
Strange that God
and my ambition
should have given me
this privilege,
to tread that field of flowers
above this church –
enshrined, remembered,
there to make it clear
that Paschal is no desecrator
of the sacred image,
and to show posterity
that we the Popes can praise,
despite Armenian barbarians
who'd strip their church walls white.
I will not have it said
that I support
such murderers of faith.
And what if they should
call me egoistic?
This would not offend.
It is to glory that I bend
my knees among the flowers
and listen to the milky
phrasings of those angels.

O Madonna, Queen of Heaven,
you have honoured me!
My little church is filled
with your dark presence
and your angels are its music.

Limbo Church

In San Clemente, Rome, where a 4th–11th century church lies beneath the 12th century upper church above a 2nd century Mithraic temple.

I turn half-sceptic
in the half-light (seeping damp)
of San Clemente's under-church.
Old frescoes
falter in the dusk.
A Christ with hand raised, blessing,
gazes off remotely
to the dark of death.
Somewhere a child
is rescued from a sea.
Clemente's relics,
watched by a pope,
are borne to rest.
While St. Alexis
dies unknown in his parents' home,
there is close by
this brown-eyed jewelled head –
the Empress-Madonna,
lapped with child – that stares
beyond her world,
to where another Christ
(the ovalled Redeemer),
leaning down, leads Adam out
from where small faces
cry unheard for justice.
Here I stop, drawn close,
my own face white as theirs –
not of the elect, far gone,
forgotten in crime perhaps.
This Christ (no time to waste)

has turned his cheek unheeding.
Though his white foot
treads down that red Satan,
it is not for us, the watchers.
An evacuation is at hand,
and Adam listlessly submits.
Too late, by Christ, too late!
To have to wait that long,
locked in that devil's anteroom,
for someone who might come
and, coming, takes one Adam out.
Better not to –
better not to think of that.
I turn relieved to words –
a man's words,
uttered in the common tongue,
that put these limbo fears to shame.

'Fili dele pute traite.'

Gulled by the saint
Sissinius shouts.

*'Gosmari, Albertel, traite.
Fallite dereto colo palo.'*

Hinting flesh and light, lost speech,
these sons of harlots sweat.
And in the dark I welcome them.
They bring a stubborn sense
of non-acceptance
to this shadowy half-world
where the spirit whimpers –
underneath which
a crude nude Mithras in his niche

stands sexed for triumph,
and set out to tempt above,
the Tree of Life
(enclosing shepherd, sheep and ram)
curls richly around
the angular
crossed godhead Christ.

'*Fili dele pute traite,*' '*Gosmari, Albertel, traite. Fallite dereto colo palo*' –
These vernacular injunctions are painted on the walls beside the images. They are among the first Italian words to appear inside a church of the 11th century.

The Toll

1

Death hovers black behind the eye,
stares gnomic from the wasted face.
'You see what I'm reduced to, Chris.'
It hardly seems conceivable
that this could be the man I'd known
two years before, here in Rome –
tall, quick in talk, assured,
resilient, the elegant host.
He glances up at me and grips my hand,
lips quivering, eyes deep-sunk,
harsh with knowledge. *'Not Gianfranco,
not Gianfranco!'* This emaciated ghost?
'Of course,' I murmur. *'You've not changed.'*
But he knows – death eating outward
to deprive him inch by inch of self;
the will besieged, forced closer in;
that confidence and pride in health
now broken, sapped, become a shrivelled
mockery; the smile a grin,
the gesture a thin bird-clutch,
the voice a plaintive whimper
from the bone and skin.

2

He leaves us here distrusting,
ransacked, uninsured
against what this death strips us of.
I think of lake-dark shadows,
Trevignano under the trees,
his children wild as Pan's;

the house on that high hill;
the mausoleum-symbol, white,
of Rome beyond the cypress-black;
and afterwards, unordered
in the wake of emptiness,
a door that opens to a black abyss;
an alley with obscene graffiti;
the shut stare of a paranoiac;
birds flying desperately nowhere.

Not of Siestas

Macerata, Marche, Italy

Snow is a fact, even in Italy:
whiteness, the sealed earth, streets of brown slush.
Lying so thick along the branches of trees
it makes its treacherously pretty patterns,
turning to monochrome the Marche colours.

But isn't this merely a joke,
a sick pretence, a trick?

Going to work, I gaze at the stunned white fields.
An Air Force captain plays with snowballs in the bus.
In the smoky classroom
one of my pupils (Naples-born)
stares at the snow, and wide-eyed tells me
that he's never seen it snow before.
I glance at him, he pouts a smile and blinks.
I do not share his dazzled surprise. Outside
(even Naples lies three inches under snow)
the white cold grips, it is no facile topic;
and there's no escape. Home in the house after lunch,
in fireless rooms the stone floors freeze – and I,
sitting at the desk (for this meridian
is not of siestas) am gripped by the zero winter.

A Letter at Dusk

I break the seal of the letter and
glance out to sea. The Spring dusk, settling,
brings flat calm, and on the page the ink
goes black as I read. *'We miss you here.'*

The Mediterranean twilight
holds its breath, and I am a stranger
caught before masts and lobster-pots, the
glaring eye on a *Cleopatra*
hulk. (The news from home is someone's ill,
it's cold.) *'And what are you doing now?'*

The question reaches me across the
lag of time, a small diminishing
echo in my head – too late, too late.
This Anzio calm will have vanished,
I'll be in my room in Rome with night
and the noisy traffic around me
before I'll have time to answer back.

A few minutes more and I shall leave
this waterfront to its silences,
and the darkening sea will go on
lapping at the wharf as it must have
even while the guns of those beachhead
landings hammered the town; as after;
as now. And into the blackening
campagna I'll drive with my letter,
trying to think of how to reply,
while this waterfront quiet recedes
and is lost beneath a Roman sky.

The Aftermath

Pompeii, south of Naples

Hard to think back.
Now you smile and come to me,
today in Pompeii.
And I can think of nothing
but this present present,
with our daughter
dwarfed beneath a dancing faun.
Now the stones seem flowers
in some formal garden run to seed.
It seems improbable
this riot could have been
preceded by Vesuvian fire.
Nothing but a Pliny story
here among the birds,
where green chokes stone,
sends tendrils
clutching up at columns
in the lesser courtyards.
Now our mood
defines the Pompeii legends
as a background
to the private world
we'd brought in with us,
histories changing every moment
with each move we make,
a shifting record
whose uncertainties and clarities
this stopped world frames.
And even smiles, a casual word,
our daughter running at us
out of ruined shops,

are more akin to those green tongues
that thrust up through mosaic
than to streets of calcined stone,
that crumpled dog we'd seen.
The aftermath of devastation
is, it seems, this fruitfulness.
It is the sun, the air, the light,
the rising saps
of earth and flesh that triumph,
where green killers stalk the streets,
pull vestiges apart;
where couples scrawl their names
through hearts on stone,
and walking hand in hand,
we move contained
above the roots of our shared world.

Affirmatives

Six days away, beyond the proofs of love,
I compensate with work and cold night walks
along Livorno's stormy seafront – prone
to doubts, exultant, taut, alone.
And later, out on Populonia's bared hill
on a January Sunday in the sun,
treading bits of broken life, these vestiges
and threads above the terraced olives,
I could fix the distances of sea and shore
as constancies between death's stopped notes, held
high up and uncorrupted as time sheds its moments.
While down there below, beyond this strand of black
volcanic sand, stone circles seem the insignia
of death's command upon this singing world –
that water, that black island riding time,
the ocean landless westward and its meeting sky:
beyond possession or inheritance, surviving
the collapse of human experiment unimpaired.

On this ridge of broken land, above the blue,
with a fragment of the vanished city in my hand –
gift of an instant scooped from the earth,
of ribbed impasto, black-patched, pink – I stand
linked back through nine long days of absence
to the essences of loving, re-affirmed by the touch
and weight of these containing actualities.

Question of Truth's Absence

The camera's eye records the image
exact and dead: the gesture
that was movement frozen out of time:
the glance deceived into perversion
of its evanescent form.
                            From the film
an unknown face, like yours
intact in feature, stares or smiles,
usurping the instant –
a congealed stiff mask
tricked out in white on black,
the smile arranged as though a skilled
mortician had touched up a corpse.

The similitude of someone you were then;
but not you, then or now. Between you,
or between two moments of you;
as it were, a shadow made secure.

No-Man's Land

It was suddenly
not any longer
what it once
could safely be considered –
a remote and abstract
other world.

Now I could sense it
somewhere
there ahead
like a shoreline
looming out of fog.

'And if you
think you have the time,
still journeying,
to get yourself
prepared for it,
who knows?
It may be coming
sooner than you think,
with the lights of the port
swimming close
across the water.

Soon, you understand,
you're going to
have to disembark.
And when the moment comes
there'll be no choice.
You'll find yourself
confronted with some kind of
no-man's land.'

Islands of the Mind

'Sir, I am vex'd.' – The Tempest, IV:1

Consider the epilogue's anguished appeal
for release from the bondage of craft.
It gets at us, that valedictory assault
upon the hidden contradictions of reality:
what Prospero contrives with his books,
conjuring renewal from a dislocated world.

But what are we to make of it – this unkempt isle
caught under the spell of an autocrat's mind?

And how are we, this late, to reconcile
what Prospero's occult dabbling made of it?

There are things that have to be spelled out
beyond what one man's dubious magic signifies,
even as we watch him forced to adjust
his harnessing of history and nature
to a world he thought he'd triumphed over.
This, with its usurpers and its cheats,
its Calibans tormented by their dreams,
we know Miranda's wide-eyed vision,
blank with trust, can be no answer to.
And Prospero, who knows it too but has to settle
for the present's reconciliations, knows
he has no power to shape the future,
but must give it over to the untried young.

And what of us, who find ourselves confronted
by the powder-keg results of humanist experiment,
living in a post-millennium world
transformed by the terrorist frenzies of war

and the wizardry of science into fissionable doubt
which, treading the moon to dust, has left us here –
'all torment, trouble, wonder and amazement' –
on the threshold of the unforeseeable,
questioning and teasing all our values out?

Caliban

'Alchemists keep skulls.' — TONY HARRISON

He knows it too,
sunk deep in matter,
mud-spattered, slow,
slurred in speech; has learned
that much and more;
has seen the way
the island's climate's
made to obey
the murmured spells
of the man in the cloak
with his stick and his books.
But though he resents
being pushed about and beaten
and sworn at and shamed,
he cannot work it out.
'This island's mine,' he says,
but gets confused by dreaming
how it speaks to him
of what it shares
and what possession means.
Although it's his by birth,
he has no grasp of that.
What he cannot get at
is the mind's control,
its artifice, its Ariel magic –
all his instincts tell him
he's powerless to break.

Witnesses

From the site of the ancient city of Tarquinii – 'once, it may be, the chief in all Italy – the metropolis of the Etruscan Confederation.'
— GEORGE DENNIS: Cities and Cemeteries of Etruria

These are the roots that speak from the roots,
embedded in the trampled earth of centuries,
worked by generations of inheritors.
Though many have forgotten or have ceased
to care, the stones remain, the broken terraces,
the flattened hilltop, the wind-smoothed spur,
as witnesses to all that stands for struggle –
here today across two thousand years and more –
for what gives dignity of place its place.

Here I stand on this Tarquinian plateau,
ploughed and ploughed, as one who listens,
hears in this cleared world the voices of the dead.
And turning to the half-buried wall, I watch
its builders strain to lift and fit the stones,
their silence glancing through me into sunlight.

From a tuft of unploughed grass at the field's edge
I drag into the open a terracotta foot,
its colour still discernible on the clay –
hollow, sandaled, red at the ankle, fragment
of a vanished god. Surviving twenty centuries,
so casually discarded, still it keeps the imprint
of the mould that fired the body it supported,
witness to an unknown craftsman's care.

I take the weight of it, try to imagine
this figure up on its plinth in a city street,
where earth and grass now rule. But as I turn it,
fingering the surface of the clay, it's not of gods
or of hierarchic order I think, but of those
without whose skills no cities can be built.

What Survives

This is not the answer. What you want
goes stretching back and back,
remains to challenge all that silences
beyond indifference, conquering neglect –
the proofs of quest, the foolproof signs
of struggle pitched against the odds.
And what survives from all that's lost
is there to work with, build on, make –
with words, these faltering words, that would speak,
if they could, the difficult music of truth.

You cannot ask for better tools to work with
or to trust, though words are not the answer,
any more than grass or trees or stones that chart the sun,
since every proof is evidence of change,
and marks the hiss and curve we move through
as we take the new, the unknown, track.

Things Taking their Course

Let things take their course then, as they will,
rain or shine. The rhythm of the Gulf Stream,
the North Pole's melting ice-cap, can't be stopped;
our days are numbered. So: 'What's to be done?'
I don't have Lenin's grasp of things; the world's
moved on from those few months at the start
of the last century when history was open
to the kind of revolutionary transformation
Lenin spent so many years preparing for.

The question remains though – after the fall,
after the failure of the Leninist vision,
even if the capitalists think,
in a world unstable and irrationalist,
it's only armed democracy can win.

That isn't the agenda some of us had planned.
The Bush-fire consequences of the fall
have brought the trumpets and the war-drums back,
a recrudescent braying of the market law
we might have hoped to counteract
with something other than this money-system
which determines how the course will run.
And what if, pitching in, you choose to swim
against the current? Who's got strength enough
to keep that up and not get swept downstream?

And yet to let things take their course must be
to take the Lemming path (as the Gulf Stream slows)
towards catastrophe. And this we have to fight
with instruments by which to measure gains and losses,
overcoming greed. Not 'after me the deluge',
but in the dialectic Leninist sense –

not simply 'things in themselves', but 'things for us' –
to make resources work for the social wealth
by which we can agree to share its riches.
Where that ended (Stalin's murderous legacy,
collapsing on itself) isn't the end of the course,
which has a long way yet to run. And maybe one day
it will give us back the power to *get* things done.

A Country Millimetres Deep

It is the smell and stain of grass and pond-weed:
   asphalt beaten by the sun:
      rotting apples
   in an empty garage-barn:
seas that pound the beaches unchecked:
   coal-grit, rain and paper:
fear of the bully on a tarmac ice-run:
voices, faces – Farley, Bloom and Drewitt, Gould:
   that Stuka-bird berserk and lethal
   raking a discarded bicycle:
and leaning out upon the window-sill,
   a boy in a summer suburb
looking for something or somebody still.

It is the chill of misty waiting-rooms:
a queue beyond the Science building:
   Lear in a late-mall dispute:
Mozart, Schubert, Schumann stumbled at.

      I cannot separate
   the voices on the stairway,
   the hissing of the wired sea,
   the moment of the Sarabande;
   beyond me as the music stops,
   those Mastersinger skies
   at midnight in a Sussex June;
      or how the talk
   moved through so many phases
to the silence of the tracking hand,
      upon you,
waking to a universe of journeyings.

That tiny cottage on the Exe
where my timidity was cured;
where lovers coupled hungrily
   against the odds, as now –
the blood alert, as now, to thresholds
   in the guessing dark of love.

You cannot hear the sound of that –
   the fingertips upon the lips,
   the hand upon the hand;
or on the slopes above the village,
sunset glittering upon the river's mouth,
   my tutress' downy belly –
she the maker leading me to contours
     that have turned
these long and slowing folds of green
   to haunted song.

Like ritual figures on a figured vase
   the creatures in my head
tread silently within their circles,
   and in slow procession,
     as in dream,
   determine what I am.

The Invitation

    No song
is ever unambiguous.
As at the edge of the dark we move,
shadowing daylight.
    The hidden valleys
that go on producing
    waste no time
    elucidating.
Though the sun returns,
    it comes
to underline the rhythms
    of the dying.

Watching the ritual
demotion of the trees,
we have to let it go,
stepping from the wreckage
    as the seasons do,
discarding winnings to renew.

    For this I wait,
as the buried white roots
    wait in earth.
No chance manoeuvres in the mind,
no charting of the void,
    can reassure.
It is the dance of the dancers
on the edge of darkness
    I am waiting for –

    the invitation,
the confirming welcome by which
    (time turned music)
    one is asked
to take one's killing habits off,
and join the dancers
on the floor of life.